Feng Shui Today

A 9-Step Guide

Easy ~ Practical ~ Effective

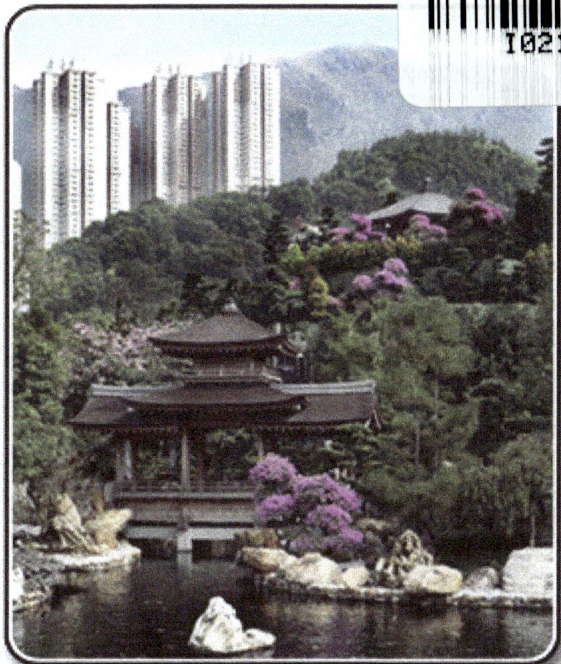

Alex Hartwell
Rhainey Watts-Cunningham

HenschelHAUS Publishing, Inc.
Milwaukee, Wisconsin

Published by
HenschelHAUS Publishing, Inc.
www.henschelHAUSbooks.com

ISBN: 978159598-542-2
E-ISBN: 978159598-616-0
LCCN: 2017905941

Illustrations / Diagrams by Alexis Ruzell

Printed in the United States of America.

A portion of the proceeds from the sale of this book
goes to support homeless shelters.

What others are saying about Feng Shui Today:

"Feng Shui was confusing to me until Alex
and Rhainey helped me apply the steps."
—Stacey K.

"My first consultation with Rhainey and Alex
helped me with my business,
which had slowed down."
—Lenaye M.

"It was easy to use the 9 steps to balance
our home and we were surprised at how
much improvement occurred."
—Selena & James G.

"Feng Shui for our home helped
mend our family relationships."
—John and Susan M.

"Soon after my Feng Shui consultation,
my health showed noticeable improvements."
—Olivia J.

"These 9 steps are easy to follow
and implement."
—Mark R.

Contents

Preface

Today, there is a growing awareness of systems and methods, like Reiki, acupuncture, yoga, meditation, sound healing and biofeedback, that utilize "energy" not currently measurable with scientific means. In Feng Shui, this unseen energy is referred to as *chi* or *life force energy*.

Feng Shui uses cures and adjustments to modify this kind of energy in order to bring about balance, harmony, and desired changes in someone's life. Feng Shui can be compared to acupuncture, in that energy pathways in the home are similar to energy meridians in the body. Feng Shui cures can be related to acupuncture needles; both are strategically placed to modify the energy flow, increase vitality, and support positive changes.

People are now more open to Feng Shui and other energy-based systems than ever before, as they look for ways to bring balance to their lives and better align with that part of themselves that creates a life of connection and ease.

We would like to thank our clients who invite us into their homes and businesses and trust us with their goals and dreams. Our experiences with them have helped us write this book.

Thank you,

Alex Hartwell

Rhainey Watts-Cunningham

Introduction

This book was written to provide simple and easy steps for its readers to understand and use Feng Shui to the best advantage for their home, business, or life. Throughout this book, when we use the word "home," it can also apply to an apartment, office space or building.

Feng Shui is often confused with interior design or known only in terms of paint selection, moving furniture around, or placing fountains here or there. We have heard frequently from clients that they have found Feng Shui books to be confusing and sometimes conflicting. Often, there are attempts to use Feng Shui cures that can actually make things worse, instead of better, because overall balance is not taken into consideration.

To help remedy these issues, based on our practice and experience, we have selected nine basic areas of focus—or steps—with adjustments that are easy to implement and essential to achieving energetic balance in a space. Creating balance in this way makes the biggest difference in achieving life goals.

In the following chapters, we explore these basic approaches as the organizational foundation of good Feng Shui.

Feng Shui Today devotes a chapter to each of these basic focus areas or steps, describing potential problems and how to fix them. Examples provided in the book of problems in these areas are just a few of the many possible ways issues could manifest from an imbalance.

Step 1 is devoted to Run-thrus, one of the more serious Feng Shui problems a home can have.

Steps 2 and 3 introduce the ideas of Physical and Electrical Balance to a space.

Step 4 looks at the Bagua as a tool to help with restoring balance to a home.

Step 5 looks at Elemental Balance.

Steps 6 and 7 explore singular elements, such as stairways and angles, as potentially detrimental to energy flow within a home.

Step 8 examines the exterior of the space, including its entry ways and the balance of the lot.

Step 9 covers selection and installation of cures and enhancements.

The final chapters cover useful ideas to use along with Feng Shui, as well as additional considerations.

When reading this book and benefiting from the information presented, it is helpful to have or create a floor plan of your own space. The legend below identifies items used to represent cures and items.

In addition to guiding you through the Feng Shui process, our intent is to help demystify Feng Shui and make it easy and enjoyable for you to utilize, implement and understand.

Have Fun!

Legend of Symbols Used in this Book

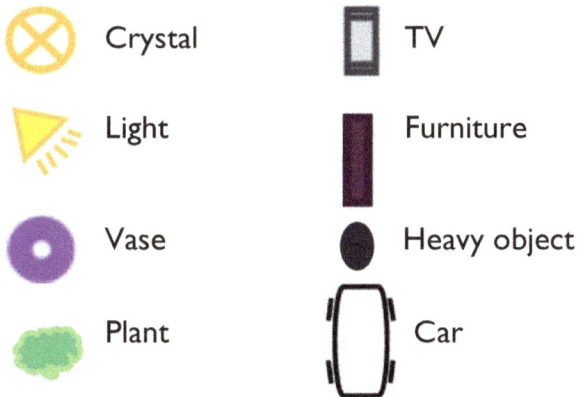

⊗	Crystal	▯	TV
◁	Light	▮	Furniture
◉	Vase	●	Heavy object
☘	Plant	⬭	Car

Fig. 1. Ideal Site

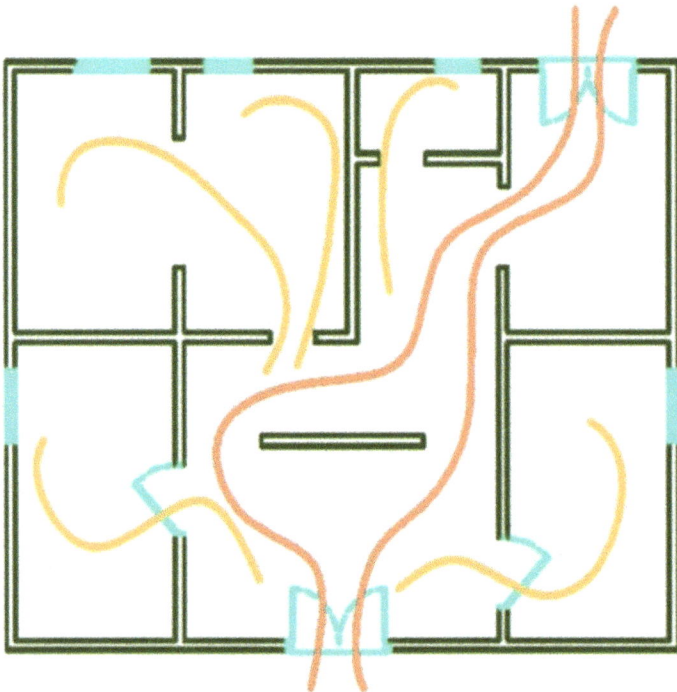

Fig. 2. Meandering Energy

Step 1
Run-thrus — The Primary Issue

O riginally, Feng Shui developed from a search for the ideal location for farmland in China. The search entailed evaluating the surrounding topography and geography of a site for the contribution of its physical and energetic components. An ideal site was considered to be a home situated halfway up a hill, facing south, overseeing a river (Fig. 1). This kind of site would allow for nourishment of the land from optimal sunshine, easy access to water, and protection from harsh winds. Over time, that process of looking at a property has been translated into methods of assessing a present-day home site.

Ideally, energy moves like a gentle meandering river throughout a home or property, nourishing every part of it equally (Fig. 2). In analyzing a home site today, we look at the degree to which the energy moves in this way.

Many Feng Shui corrections are directly related to problems with the flow of this energy. The most serious of these issues we describe as a "Run-thru." A Run-thru is a straight and uninterrupted pathway where energy moves too rapidly through a home. Looking at Run-thrus and energy pathways is the first step we take to Feng Shui a home.

The most significant or Primary Run-thru in a home occurs when the back door or a back window is directly opposite the front door and the pathway between the two is unobstructed (Fig. 3). The Run-thru creates a rushing river

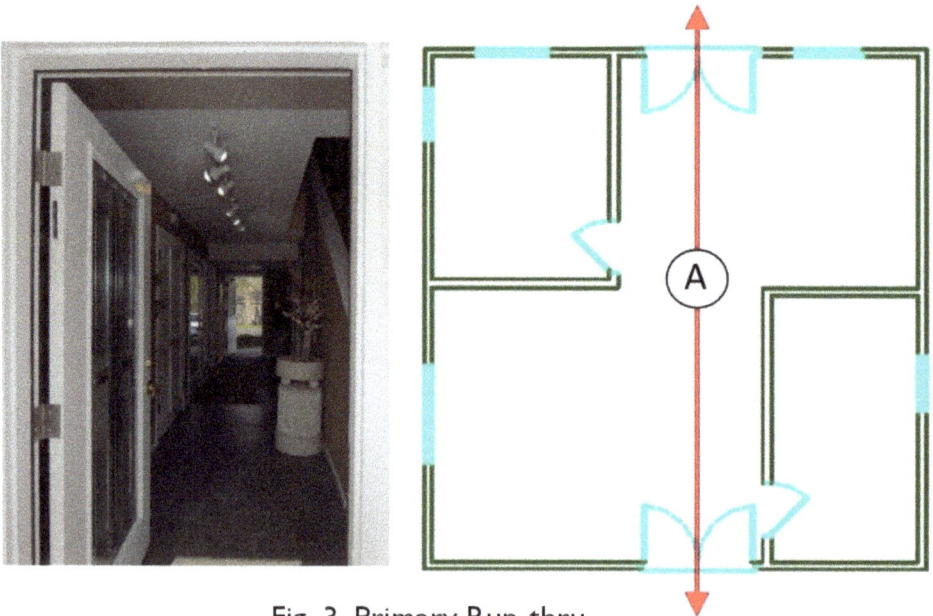

Fig. 3. Primary Run-thru

effect, which drains energy and vitality from the surrounding rooms, as well as energy from the homeowner's life. When the energy flows in the front door and out the back door or window in this way, it doesn't nourish other parts of the home, draining resources like money, support, and relationship. Also, clutter can gather as the homeowners unconsciously try to ground themselves and slow the energy of the river effect down by placing objects in and around the pathway.

In correcting or "curing" a Run-thru, the intent is to interrupt the rushing energy so that it meanders and nourishes more of the home. The nourishment then can support the flow of money, improve relationships and benefit other life goals. Clutter that is no longer being used to modify the Run-thru is managed more easily.

Fig. 4. Secondary Run–thru

Other types of Run-thrus, called Secondary Run-thrus, occur when there is an interior door opposite a window, or two windows opposite each other (Fig. 4). Additionally, a Run-thru is created when an uninterrupted hallway or space is 30 feet or longer. These Run-thrus affect the life areas of the home that they are involved with (Fig. 5). Specifically, if they occur in the Wealth, Health, or Relationship Areas, correcting them is generally of greater interest to the average property owner. (See Bagua, Step 4).

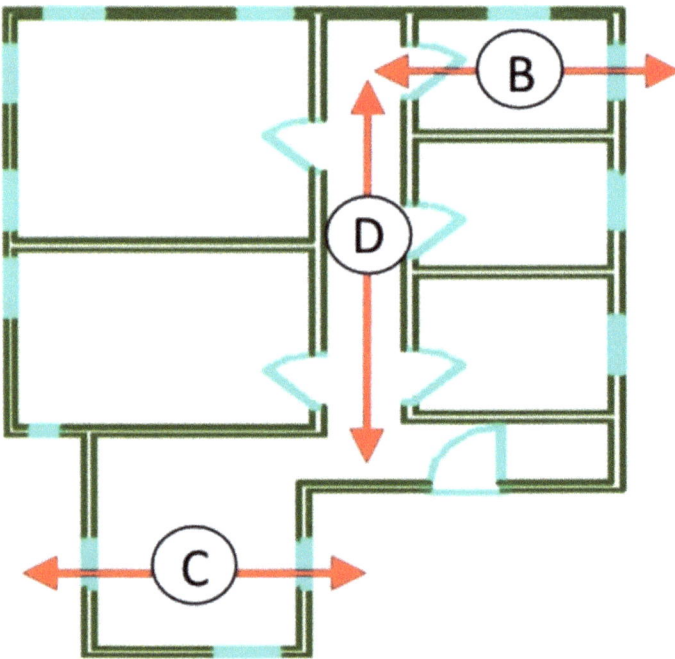

Fig. 5. Secondary Run-thrus

The traditional Feng Shui interrupter for a Primary Run-thru is to hang a faceted crystal ball in the Run-thru pathway (Fig. 6). Other ways to adjust the energy flow include placing furniture, large plants, pots, decorative screens, a substantial object, an area rug, lighting, artwork or a combination of smaller items like large flower vases in and along the pathway (Fig. 7). These items are placed in a way that requires the energy to move around them, redirecting the flow to create a gentle winding effect, like the meandering river.

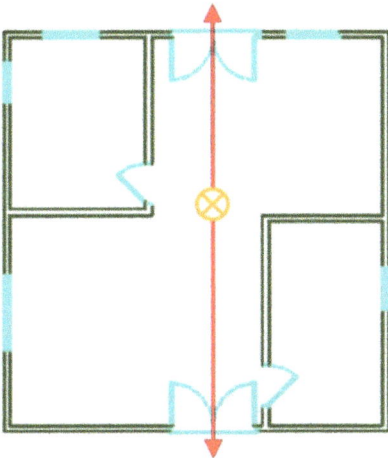

Fig. 6. Primary Run-thru
Crystal Cure

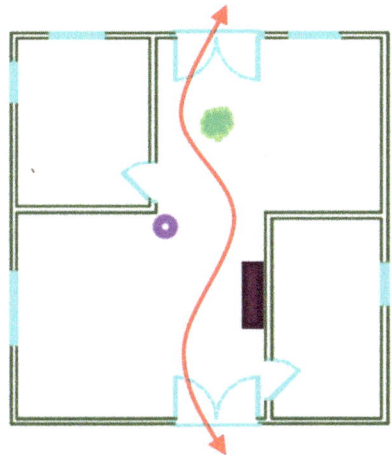

Fig. 7. Primary Run-thru
Other Cures

Secondary Run-thrus are treated in the same way, using small items and smaller crystals (Fig. 8 and 9).

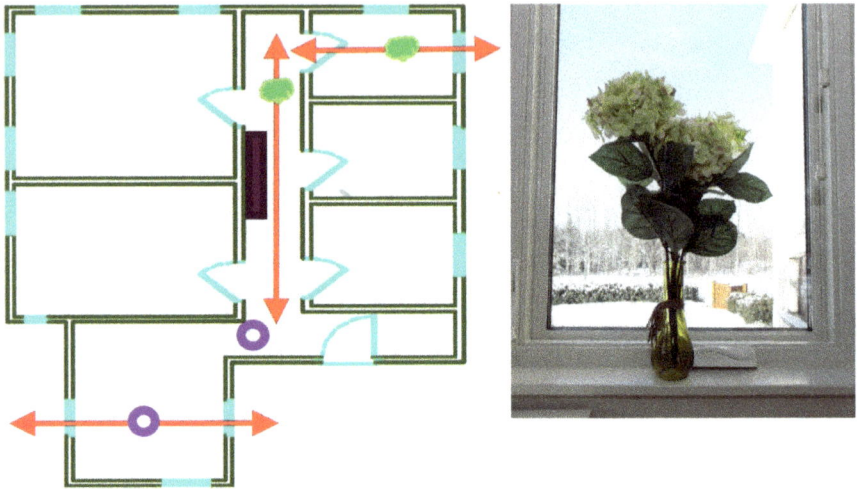

Fig. 8. Secondary Run-thru Other Cures

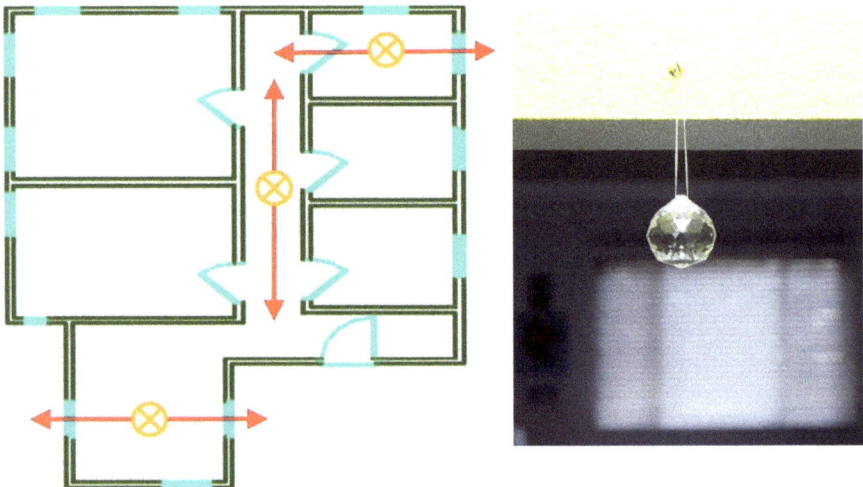

Fig. 9. Secondary Run-thru Crystal Cures

In some primary Run-thru situations, grounding objects placed at the wall edges of the Run-thru, opposite one another and about half the length of the Run-thru, can be used to modify the flow of energy. (Fig. 9a).

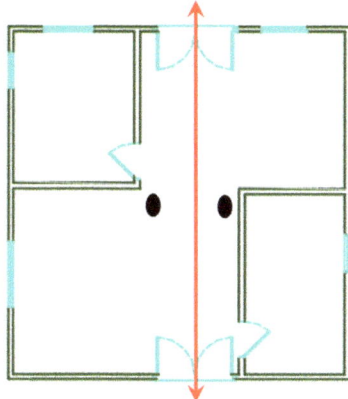

Fig. 9a: Heavy Objects

Frequently, we encounter homeowners who tell us they have read Feng Shui books and have tried to apply what they have read. In most cases, we find they miss significant issues like Run-thrus. For example, a homeowner called us and asked for our help, because he was still struggling with finances after making Feng Shui adjustments from what he had read.

Immediately upon walking into the home, it was clear to us that there was an unobstructed Run-thru from the front door to the back door without any interruptions. Soon after installing the cures, the homeowner's financial situation showed improvement.

Adjusting or curing Run-thrus, if they are present, is essential to making changes and achieving the goals you desire.

In some cases, Run-thrus can be useful and may not need treatment. For example, a Run-thru that separates a home office from the rest of the house could support healthy boundaries between family and work life.

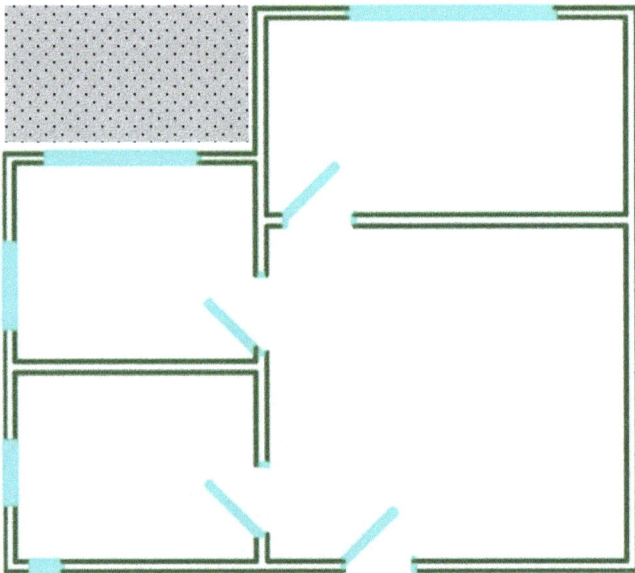

Fig. 10. Missing Area

Step 2
Missing Areas and Extensions

R estoring balance is central to the Feng Shui process. We see a direct relationship between restoring the balance of a home and creating the kind of life you want. In Feng Shui, we look at balance in terms of the Structural, Electrical and Activity aspects of a home. Structural items include Missing Areas, Extensions, angled walls and ceilings, stairways, bathrooms, garages, and Shar points.

We begin with the floor plan of the home to see if there are Missing Areas or Extensions. These are important structural issues to consider.

A Missing Area is created when a home shape or floor plan is less than an exact square or rectangle and the length of the missing space is less than one half of the length of the wall it is on (Fig. 10).

An Extension is created by the portion of the home that is left when the length of the missing space is more than one half of the wall it is on (Fig. 11).

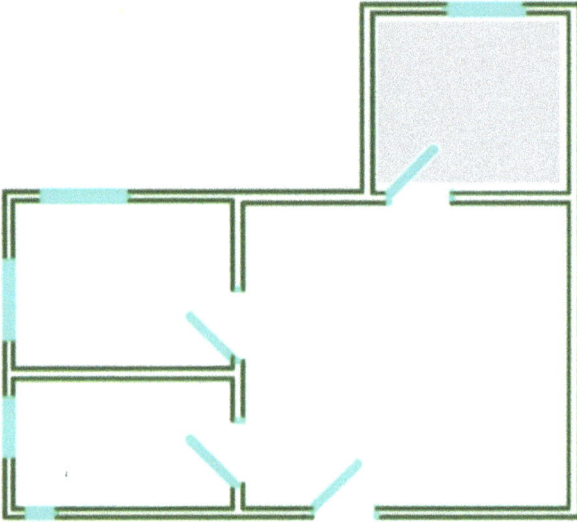

Fig. 11. Extension

Imbalances occur in a home because a Missing Area or Extension disrupts the even flow of energy in the rest of the home. Cures are used in both cases so that the Missing Area is not a detriment and so that the Extension can become a benefit.

In the case of a Missing Area (Fig. 10), a cure would be used to fill in the energy of the missing space (Fig. 12). The cure most frequently used, because it is inexpensive and easy to install, is a leaded, faceted crystal ball. The ball is hung nine inches down from the ceiling and three to nine inches out from the center of one or both of the Missing Area walls. For larger Missing Areas, it is best to cure both walls.

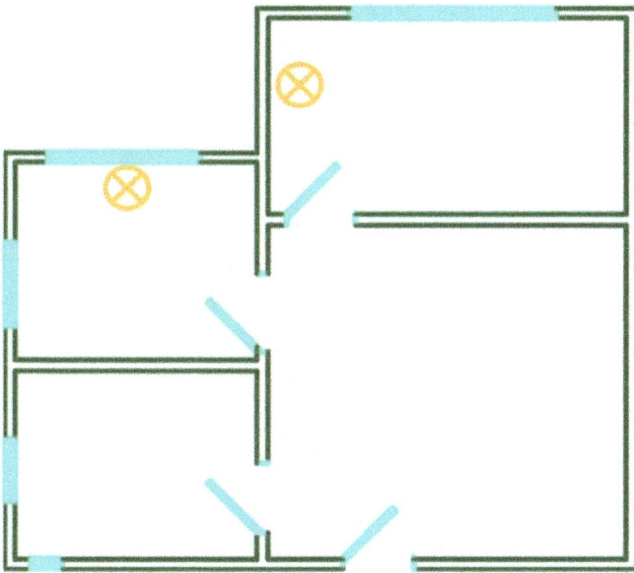

Fig. 12. Missing Area Crystal Cure

The Missing Area can also be filled in by placing a light shining back on the house exactly at the outside corner of the Missing Area (Fig. 13). Alternatively, an energizing element, like a tree, a garden, a sitting area, a large fountain, sculpture or bird-feeding area can be placed in the Missing Area.

Fig. 13. Missing Area Light Cure

In the case of an Extension (Fig. 11), a cure would be used to raise the energy of the area opposite the Extension (Fig. 14). Again, the crystal is the simplest cure and would be placed within the area equal to the size of the extension and opposite of it.

Alternatively, energetic objects, ranging from a plant to a lamp, could be placed in the same area. Cures placed at these points balance the energy of the extension. For a list of other energizing objects or cures, see Appendix A.

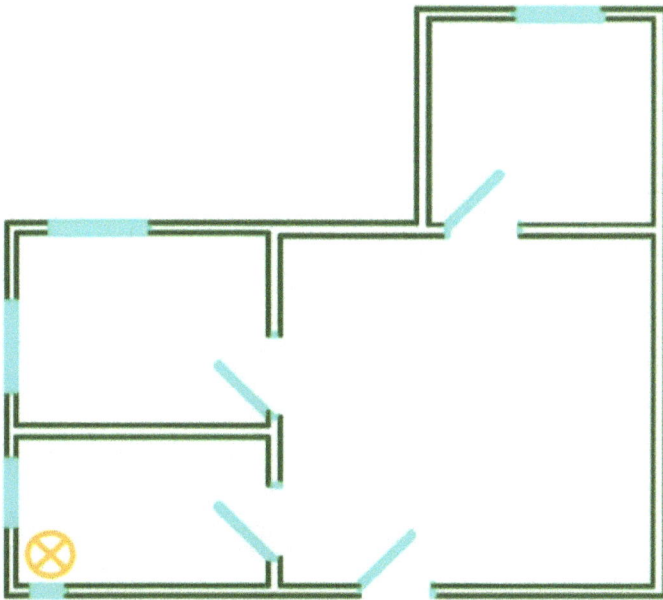

Fig. 14. Extension Crystal Cure

Figures 15 and 16 show how Feng Shui looks at which rooms are opposite of each other when considering balance. Opposites are perpendicular when in the center and diagonal when in the corners.

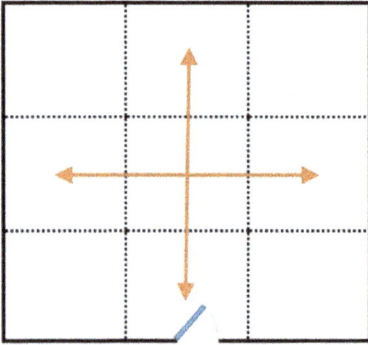

Fig. 15. Perpendicular
Opposites

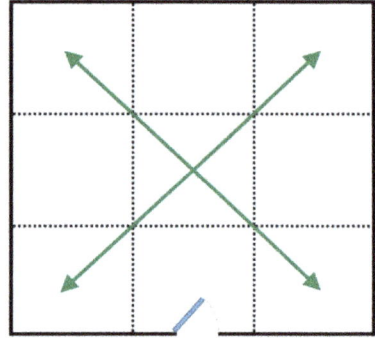

Fig. 16. Diagonal
Opposites

When structural cures are not making enough of a difference in accomplishing client goals, a crystal can be used in the center of the home to help balance out energetic differences that aren't easily quantifiable.

In one case, a family had lived in their home for 17 years without issues until they built a kitchen addition. After the remodel was complete, they began to have financial troubles that continued until their home fell into foreclosure. When they attempted to sell the home, their realtor called us to help with the sale. After studying the floor plans before and after the remodel (Fig. 17 and 18), we discovered that the remodel floor plan created a Missing Area in Wealth. (See Step 4, Bagua Life Areas.)

Cures were utilized to correct the Missing Area and helped to complete the home sale. An earlier solution could have addressed the Feng Shui problem in the first place and allowed them to keep their house.

Achieving a healthy balance can help create an environment that supports the goals of the property owner. Ease of living and enjoyment of your space are other benefits of healthy home balance.

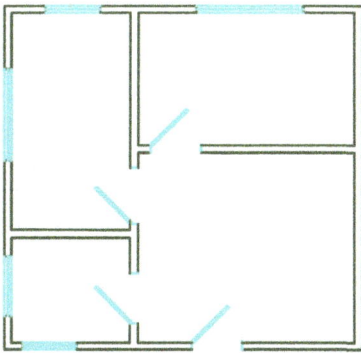

Fig. 17. Before Remodel

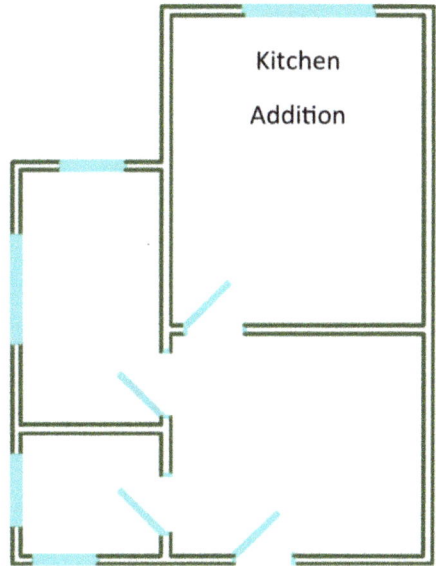

Fig. 18. After Remodel

Other Structural Elements, including Angles, Bathrooms, Stairs, Garages, and Shars are discussed in Steps 6 and 7.

Notes

....
....
....
....
....
....
....
....
....
....
....
....
....
....
....
....

Step 3
Balancing Activity and Electrical Components

Looking at the balance of Activity and Electrical levels is also important. Some examples of Activities in a home include cooking, eating, reading, sleeping and kids playing. Electrical examples include anything that is plugged in, like a lamp, a television, computer or microwave.

Imbalances occur when there are differences in Activity or Electrical levels in any of the opposite areas (Fig. 15 and 16). Again, as with Structural Balance, Step 2, the room oppositions are considered either as diagonally opposite or perpendicularly opposite each other in the house when viewing the floor plan.

Because of their energizing quality, Electrical and Activity elements need to be considered in terms of balance. For example, an imbalance of Activity occurs when

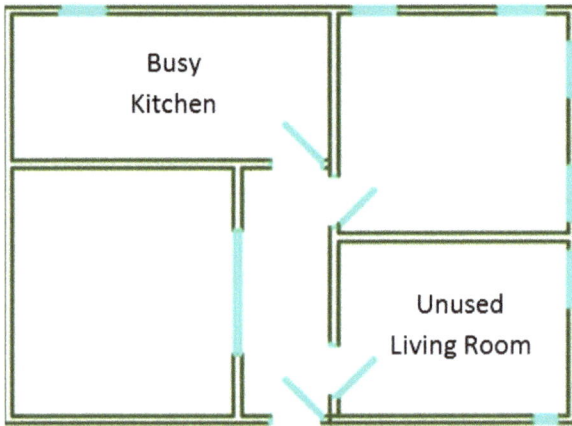

Busy
Kitchen

Unused
Living Room

Fig. 19. Activity Imbalance

an active eat-in kitchen is opposite an unused living room (Fig. 19).

An Electrical Imbalance occurs when a quiet study with a single lamp is opposite a rec room with a large television (Fig. 20). Most often, rooms have both Electrical and Activity levels involved and the balance of the combination of both needs to be taken into account. Generally,

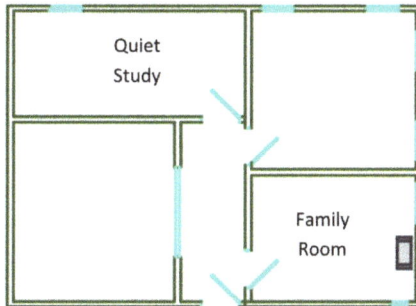

Fig. 20. Electrical Imbalance

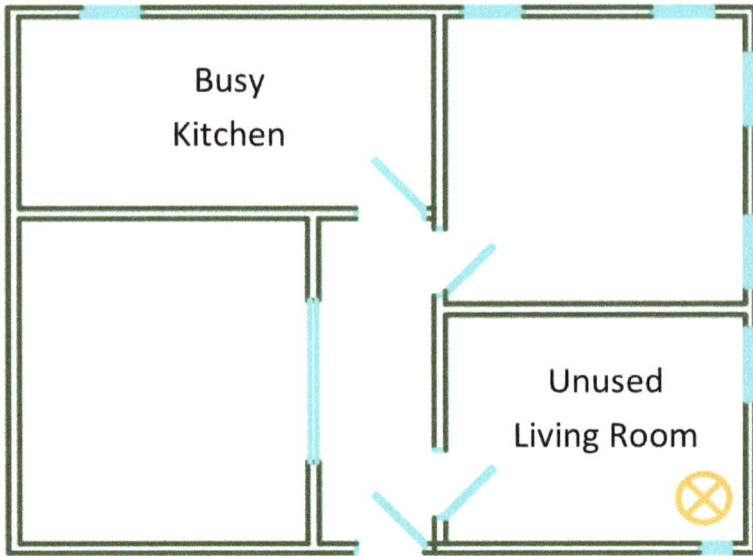

Fig. 21. Activity Imbalance Crystal Cure

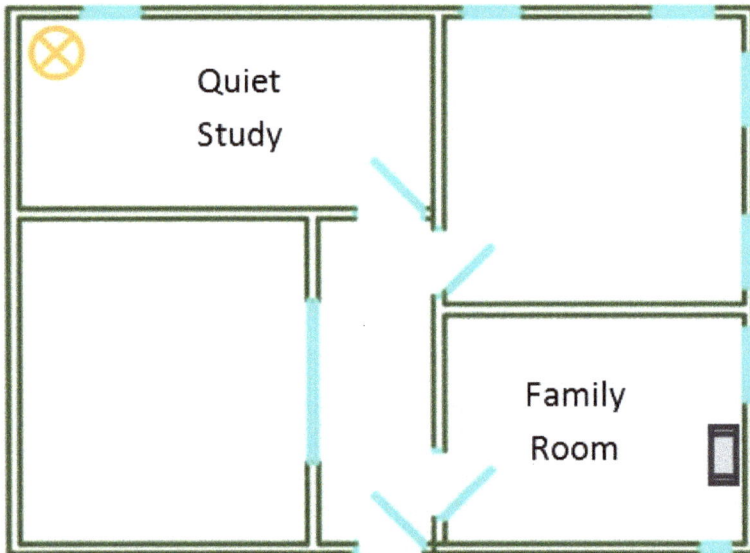

Fig. 22. Electrical Imbalance Crystal Cure

kitchens will have higher Electrical and Activity elements compared to most rooms opposing them.

Activity and Electrical levels should also be evaluated in terms of frequency and intensity. For example, a home owner who only cooks on Sundays and eats out the rest of the week, would demonstrate low cooking activity, whereas a family of four who always cooks and eats at home, would be demonstrating a high cooking activity level. A large television frequently watched has a higher level of electrical intensity than a small computer occasionally used.

Further examples of activities that might be considered in the home include animals kept in one area, bathroom activity or workshop areas. Electrical examples can also include stoves, fish tanks and air conditioners.

To cure Activity imbalances, the energy of the less active room is raised. This can be accomplished by hanging a crystal (Fig. 21). Alternatively, a light, electrical item or other cures listed in Appendix A can be used in the less active room. To cure Electrical imbalances, raise the energy of the room with less electrical charge in the same way by using a crystal (Fig. 22) or cures listed in Appendix A.

We visited a home and met a family whose goal was to improve difficult family relationships. The home had an active family room with a large television set opposite an infrequently used dining room. We had the owners hang a 40mm crystal in the center of the room over the dining room table to assist in balancing the energy of the active family room.

After several weeks, we returned to the home and were told there were improvements in the family relationships, but not as many as they were hoping for. We had them exchange the 40mm crystal with a larger 50mm crystal to further raise the energy of the dining room. This adjustment improved the balance and they soon let us know that relationships had also benefited. The subtlety of the Electrical/Activity relationship, as in this case, can require testing and reevaluation.

When Activity and Electrical cures are not completely accomplishing client goals, a crystal can be used in the center of the home to help balance out energetic differences that aren't easily quantifiable.

While balancing the energy of the first floor is primary, it is also of value to consider doing the same for a second floor, if there is one.

Notes

WEALTH & PROSPERITY	FAME & REPUTATION	RELATIONSHIP & MARRIAGE
HEALTH & FAMILY	CENTER	CREATIVITY & CHILDREN
KNOWLEDGE & SELF-CULTIVATION	CAREER	HELPFUL PEOPLE & TRAVEL

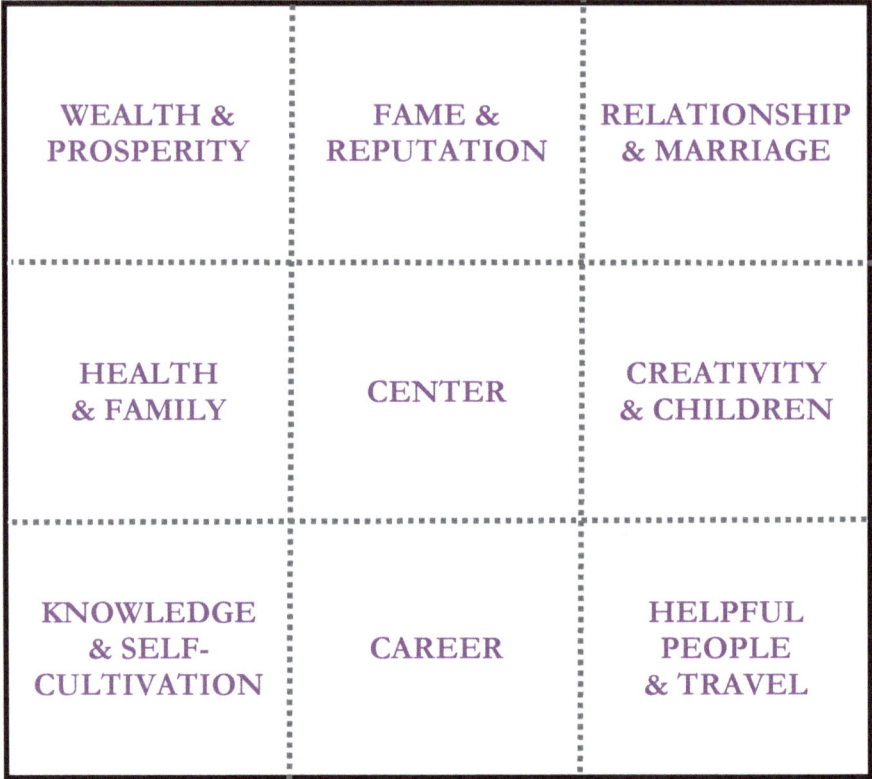

Fig. 23. Bagua Life Areas

Step 4
The Bagua

O ne of the major tools in Feng Shui is the Bagua, which was derived from the I-Ching. It is used to locate the Life Areas in the home and to focus related intentions in those areas (Fig. 23).

To find where the Life Areas are located in your home, place the Bagua map over the first floor of the home floor plan with the bottom edge in line with the main entry door of the house (Fig. 24 on page 32). (If you do not have a floor plan, draw one of your own that is to scale, in proportion, or a reasonable estimate.)

Next, line up the left side of the Bagua with the longest external wall on the left side of the house (Fig. 25 on page 32). Then stretch the Bagua to do the same, first on the right wall (Fig. 26 on page 33) and then on the back side of the house (Fig. 27 on page 33), matching the longest external wall in each case.

With the Bagua overlaying the floor plan in this way, you can see which Life Areas correspond to specific parts

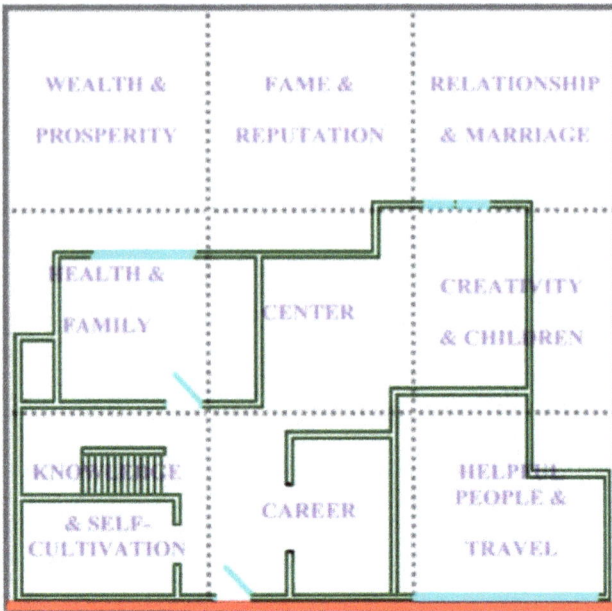

Fig. 24. Bagua in line with front door

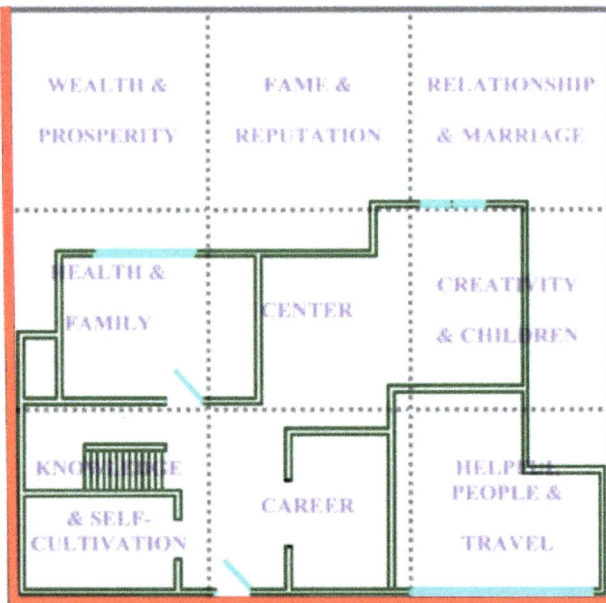

Fig. 25. Bagua left wall

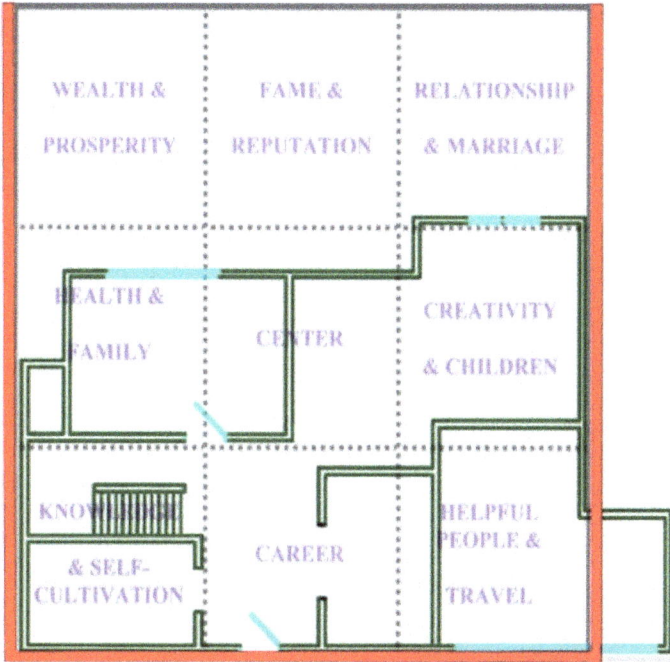

Fig. 26. Bagua right wall

WEALTH & PROSPERITY

FAME & REPUTATION

RELATIONSHIP & MARRIAGE

HEALTH & FAMILY

CENTER

CREATIVITY & CHILDREN

KNOWLEDGE & SELF-CULTIVATION

CAREER

HELPFUL PEOPLE & TRAVEL

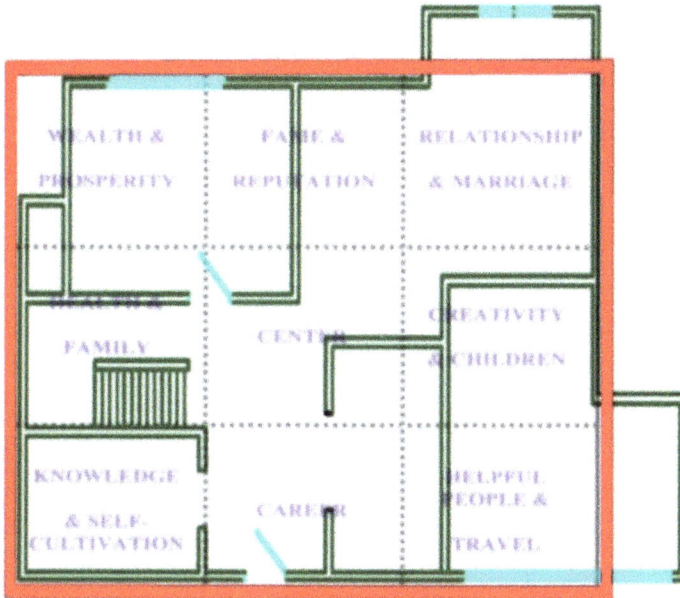

Fig. 27. Bagua back wall

WEALTH & PROSPERITY

FAME & REPUTATION

RELATIONSHIP & MARRIAGE

HEALTH & FAMILY

CENTER

CREATIVITY & CHILDREN

KNOWLEDGE & SELF-CULTIVATION

CAREER

HELPFUL PEOPLE & TRAVEL

of the home. You can also discover which Life Areas are related to a Missing Area (Fig. 28) and which areas are connected to an Extension (Fig. 29). Any portions of the Bagua that are not filled in by the house are considered Missing Areas.

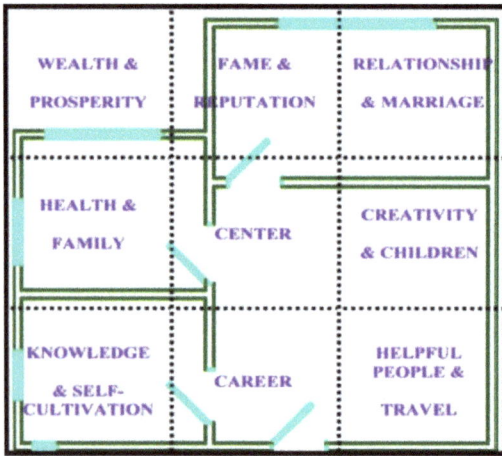

Fig. 28. Bagua Over Missing Area

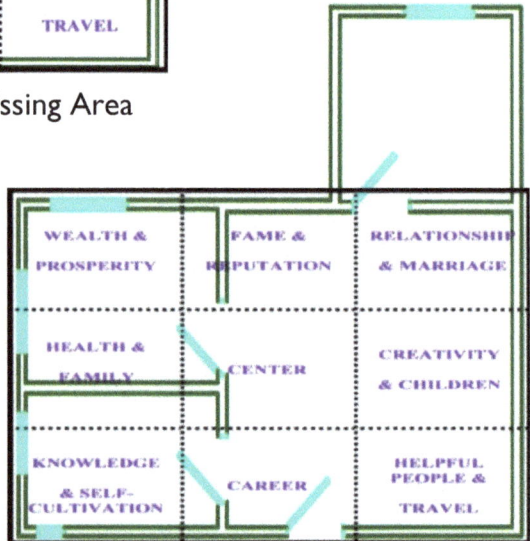

Fig. 29. Bagua Over Extension

Areas that extend out beyond the Bagua are considered Extensions. Knowing which Life Areas relate to the Missing sections or Extensions helps to see potential benefits or problems in those Life Areas or areas associated with them.

For example, a home that has an extension in the Fame Area could have a well-respected or well-known owner. If the Helpful People Area is extended, life is more likely to go smoothly because of the abundance of help available.

Extensions can add value to the Life Areas they are connected to as long as they are in balance with their opposite area. If the home has an extension in Helpful People that is not in balance with its opposite area, Wealth, it could manifest as the owners having to do everything themselves.

Missing Areas can detract value from the corresponding Life Areas if not cured. For example, if the home has a missing Wealth Area, financial troubles are likely. If some of the Helpful People Area is missing, there could be lack of cooperation among family members.

Key Life Areas are those that are most important to the owner's current life experience. For example, someone looking for a life partner would find focusing on the Relationship Area useful, someone with health problems would focus on the Health and Family Area, someone looking for a better job would look more closely at the Career Area. See Appendix C for a list of possible issues as they relate to Life Areas.

The Bagua can also be overlaid on the floor plan of the home to explore which Life Areas are affected by Electrical elements or Activity levels. Life Areas that have significant Electrical or Activity levels are energized. For example, kitchens are generally more active than other areas of the house. Having a kitchen in the Helpful People Area could indicate better relationships across the board. Family rooms can have large televisions that activate the Life Area in which they are located. If you find one in Fame, it could draw more attention to your life or career.

It is important to note that higher Electrical and Activity levels are beneficial only if they are in balance with their opposite area. For example, if the home has an often-used computer room in Wealth, but the area opposite is unused, it could manifest as a struggle to make ends meet due to the imbalance.

Although we have discussed Key Life Areas, it is important to note that the other Life Areas can have impact as well and should be examined for the degree to which they affect your goals. For example, when the goal is family harmony, you will look at the Health and Family Area, but can also consider the Relationship and Helpful

People Areas to create a comfortable sense of belonging in the family.

In another case, if the goal is increased prosperity, look at the Wealth Area and its balance with its opposite area, Helpful People. You could also consider the Career and Fame Areas that might apply in this situation.

The Center section of the Bagua is also important as it relates to all of the Life Areas and can benefit or detract from the owner's goals. Oftentimes, the center of a home lacks a grounded focus, which can detract from the owner's intent.

To adjust for this and stabilize the home, bring an item or items to the Center Area that carry some weight to them or give an impression of heaviness, like a potted plant or large floor vase. Additionally, an area rug or valued picture can be used to bring focus to the Center Area. If that is not feasible, a crystal can be hung in the approximate center of the home.

Looking at the Bagua Life Areas that are currently presenting difficulty in your life can give you information on where imbalances may be present in your home and help you determine where cures might be needed.

The Bagua can also be overlaid on the lot of the home, which will be discussed in Step 8. The important role elements play in your space as they relate to Life Areas is discussed in the next step.

Fire
RED

WEALTH & PROSPERITY	FAME & REPUTATION	RELATION-SHIP & MARRIAGE
HEALTH & FAMILY	CENTER *Earth* EARTH TONES	CREATIVITY & CHILDREN
KNOWLEDGE & SELF-CULTIVATION	CAREER	HELPFUL PEOPLE & TRAVEL

Wood
GREENS

Metal
WHITE
SILVER

Water
BLUE, BLACK

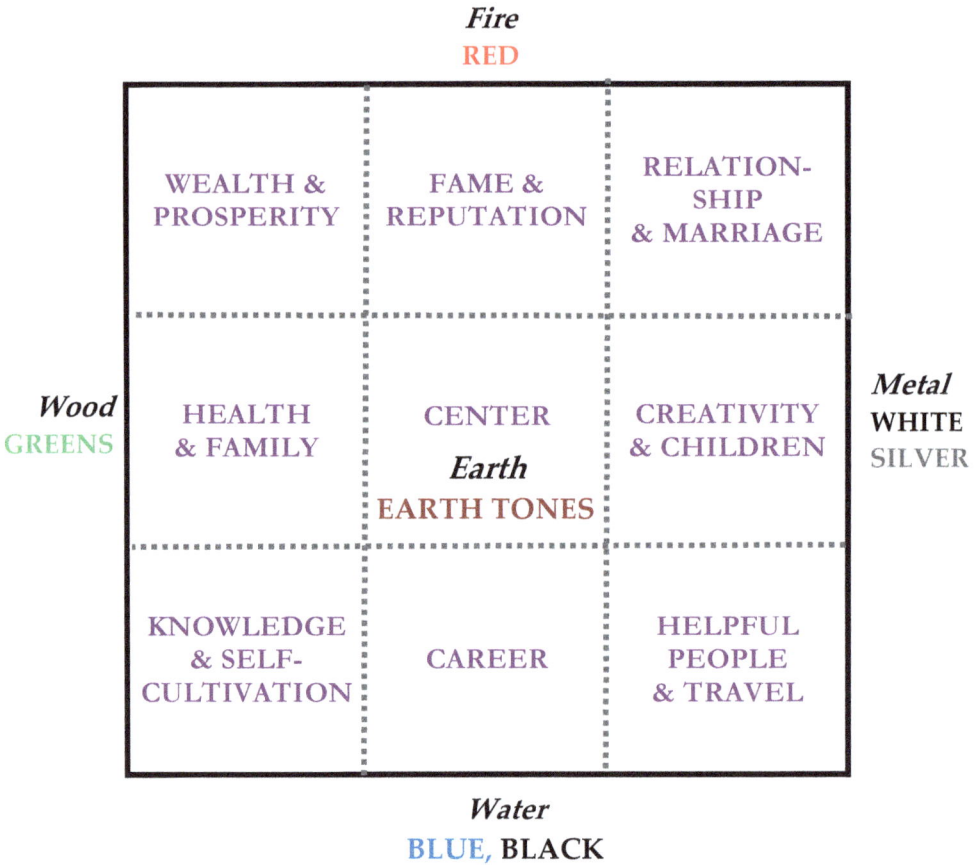

Fig. 30. Bagua with Elements

Step 5
Elemental Balance

The five elements represent the natural forces that can combine and interact in our lives in a beneficial or problematic way. They include Wood, Fire, Metal, Earth and Water.

- Wood element items include plants, flowers, trees, green colors and rectangles.

- The Fire element is represented by the colors red, bright orange, and bright yellow, as well as triangles and fire itself.

- Blues, blacks, wavy lines and water represent the Water element.

- The Metal element is represented by circles, the colors white and silver and Metal objects.

- Unglazed pottery, dirt, squares and earth tone colors represent the Earth element. (See Appendix A for more information on the elements.)

A home that has some representation of all of the elements will feel more comfortable and is more likely to support the owner's goals and dreams. Occasionally, one element may be dominant in a home. For example, a home with green décor, wood paneling and many plants, has a dominant wood element. This may create an unbalanced feeling. It could be equally uncomfortable if one element is significantly lacking. For example, a home that has no earth representations could feel less grounded for the inhabitants.

Adjustments to the above examples and others can be managed by utilizing the Creative Cycle (Fig. 31) or Destructive Cycle of elements (Fig. 32).

The two cycles show the order in which individual elements enhance or reduce each other. If the Wood element is dominant in your home, look to the Destructive Cycle to see which element minimizes the effect of Wood. Metal is used to mediate the effect of Wood, so in this case, bring in metal items, silver or white colors or circular patterns.

Alternatively, reduce the amount of wood in the home or, if possible, add the elements that are lacking in proportion to the wood to achieve balance.

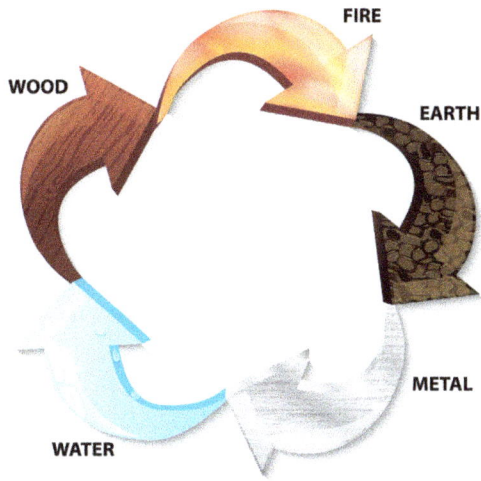

Fig. 31. Creative Cycle

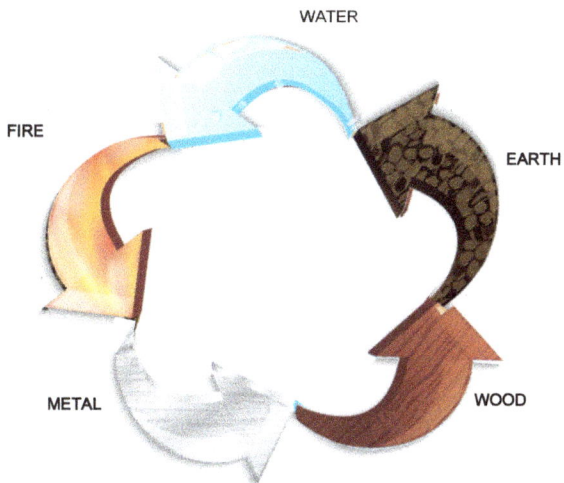

Fig. 32. Destructive Cycle

In a case of too little Earth in proportion to the other elements in a home, add more of the Earth element or support it with its enhancing element from the Creative Cycle—Fire.

The elements Fire, Water, Earth, Metal, and Wood can be located on the Bagua map, along with their natural position and colors (Fig. 30 on page 38).

In the home, we look to see if there is an element that is placed in a way that might be in conflict with the natural element of that Life Area to the detriment of personal or business goals.

An important example is when the Water element is found in the Fame Area, whose natural element is Fire. Water in the form of fish tanks, sinks, fountains, extensive blue color or wavy lines placed in the Fame Area can extinguish its fire or create steam. Pictures of waterfalls, lakes and rivers may also be detrimental in the Fame Area and invite unfavorable attention to the home owner.

This can also be seen outdoors in the lot Bagua when a swimming pool, hot tub or pond is situated in the Fame Area (see Step 8).

Another example is fireplaces, which can be frequently found in the Health and Family Area, where the natural element is Wood. This conflict could create an uneasy feeling in the homeowner or even result in illness or disease. To balance misplaced elements, either remove the offending element or use the Creative or Destructive Cycle to mitigate its effect.

We were invited to visit a home whose owner was having trouble finding a new job. In evaluating the home, we discovered the Water element to be dominant.

A bronze sculpture was visible when we entered the home. The interior colors were predominantly blue, the artwork was dominated by images of the ocean and mirrors were present throughout the home. Because mirrors are considered to be a Metal element, like the bronze sculpture, and Metal creates Water, they added to the water that was represented by the artwork and the blue interior.

We considered the excess water to be responsible for washing away the job opportunities. After reducing the number of mirrors and bringing in plants to absorb some of the water, the owner received an excellent job offer.

Notes

Notes

....
....
....
....
....
....
....
....
....
....
....
....
....
....
....
....
....
....
....
....

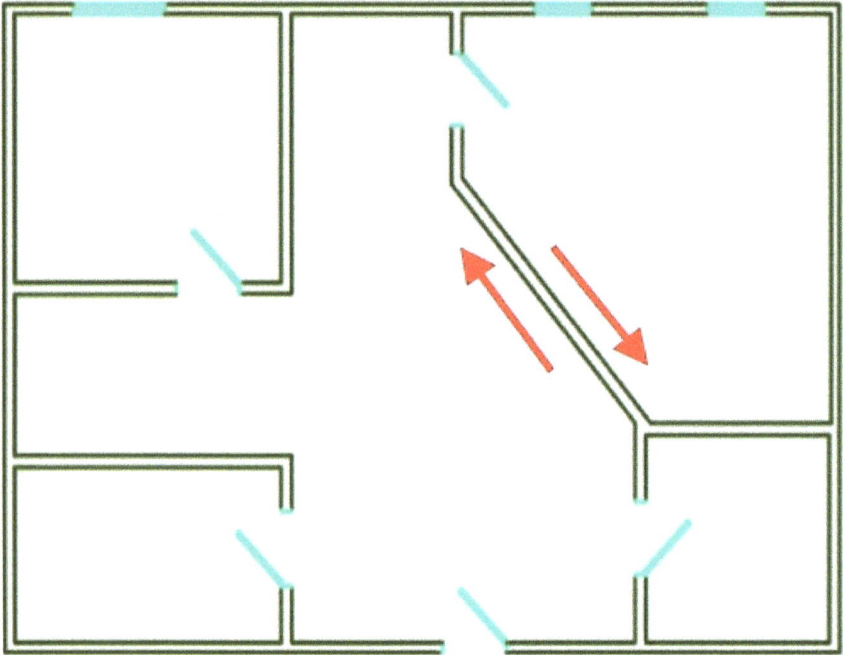

Fig. 33. Angled Walls

Step 6
Issues with
Angles and Shars

In our experience, angled walls, ceilings and doors can create significant Feng Shui problems for the Life Areas in which they occur. The energy along angled walls and ceilings flows more rapidly than along other walls, creating energetic imbalances within the entire home (Fig. 33).

Angles in the home tend to generate issues that are problematic or tricky. For example, an angled wall in Fame could manifest as problems with an owner's reputation. An angled door to a child's room could indicate health or emotional issues, as well as other possible disturbances with that child.

Cures for the angled walls bring balance to the home by slowing down the speed of flow along the angled wall so that it is more in harmony with the rest of the room. To cure angled walls, place an object centered on the wall, or at each end of the wall. Use items such as paintings, decorative vases or potted plants (live or silk).

Another option is to hang a crystal centered on the wall three to nine inches out from the wall and three to nine inches down from the ceiling.

For an angled doorway, place tiles, plaques, stenciling or artwork of some kind above both sides of the door (Fig. 34). Another option is to hang a crystal on both sides of the door three inches out from the center of the door and hanging three inches down.

Fig. 34. Angled Door with Cure

In the case of an angled ceiling (Fig. 35), place pictures or items similar to those used with the angled door intermittently along the angled surface of the ceiling with the intent to visually open up the surface and make it feel less oppressive. An angled ceiling can also be cured by installing skylights, lighting, crystals or mobiles to interrupt the effect of the angle (Fig. 36).

Points and corners generate sharp, harmful energy or what is called *Shar Chi*. In Feng Shui, a *Shar* is created

Fig. 35. Angled Ceiling

Fig. 36. Angled Ceiling Cured

Fig. 38. Shar Ceiling Edge

Fig. 37. Shar Corner

when a corner 90 degrees or less extends into a room (Fig. 37) or out from an exterior building (Fig. 39).

Other examples of Shars include pointed objects, sharp corners on furniture, or corners and edges created by changes in ceiling levels (Fig. 38). Energy extends directly out from the corner, point or edge like an arrow, negatively affecting whatever is in its path.

We look at the interior Shars for their effect on goal areas. Shars can create a variety of issues, ranging from health disturbances, arguments in relationships or troubles in the Life Areas their arrows point to.

We consider Shars created from exterior buildings or objects first, because they potentially have a stronger impact (Fig. 39). In Hong Kong, companies intentionally constructed buildings with Shars directed at their competitors' buildings in order to negatively affect those businesses. The practice got so out of hand that laws were passed against building in this way. Signage and sculpture are examples of outdoor Shars that could also be potentially harmful.

Interior Shars are cured by placing objects in front of the corners and points to block the arrow energy (Fig. 40).

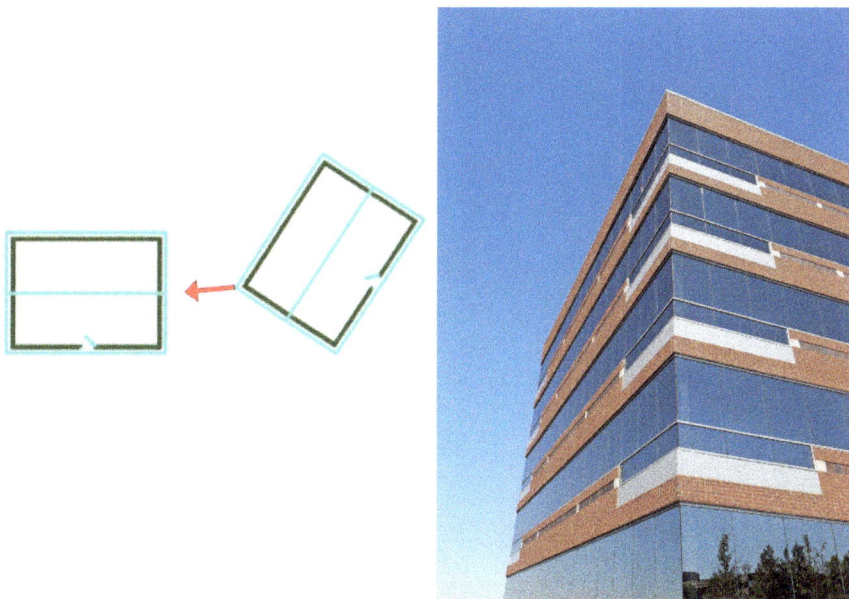

Fig. 39. Exterior Shar

Items that can be used include plants, draped fabric, corner protectors and so on. A crystal can also be hung from the ceiling off the Shar edge or point.

A change in ceiling level is cured by placing plaques, tiles, mirrors or other decorative items intermittently along the face of the drop down (Fig. 41). An exterior Shar is cured by placing an object in line with the Shar between the Shar and the house. In some cases, when larger Shars cannot be interrupted, a Bagua mirror (see Appendix A) is placed outside the home facing the offending Shar with the intent to block or interrupt the energy.

Fig. 40. Shar Corner Cure

Fig. 41. Dropped Ceiling Cure

Step 7
Bathrooms, Garages and Stairways —Further Disruptions

BATHROOMS

Wherever a bathroom is located in the house, it drains energy from the corresponding Life Area, which can affect your goals. For example, a bathroom in Wealth could drain away money. A bathroom in the Children Area could relate to fertility issues. A bathroom in the center of the home could affect any of the Life Areas.

A bathroom drain-out can be cured by hanging a crystal in the center of the bathroom to reverse the effect. Another approach would be hanging a full-length mirror on the outside of the bathroom door to "disappear" the draining effect of the bathroom.

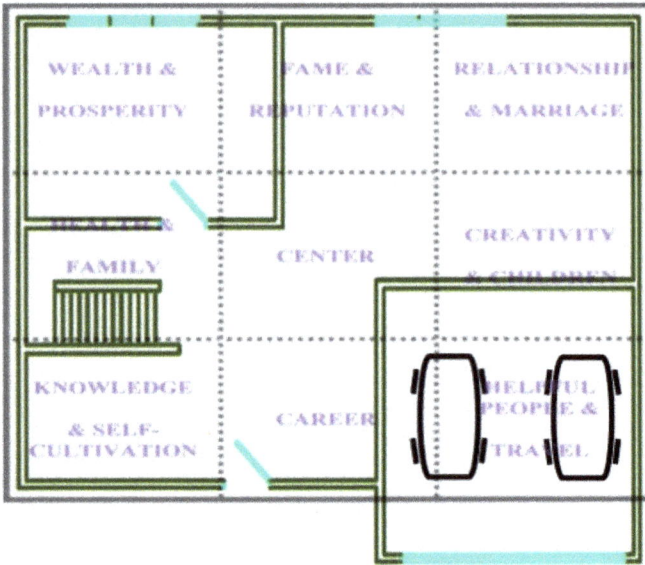

Fig. 42. Attached Garage

GARAGES

The energy flow of an attached garage is often quite different from that of the rest of the home and can create imbalances within the home.

The attached garage is treated as part of the Bagua (Fig. 42). Each Life Area within the garage needs be treated for the in-and-out energy of the cars. For example, in a home with an attached garage in the Helpful People and Travel Area, the residents could experience difficulties in that Life Area, or in the opposite areas, Wealth and Prosperity.

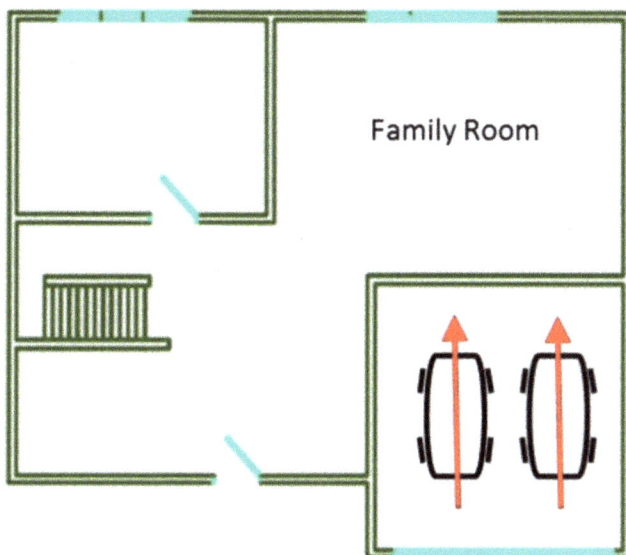

Fig 43. Car Energy into Home

When the attached garage includes Relationship, it can bring instability to the marriage. The easiest way to cure a garage is to hang a crystal in the center of each Life Area the garage covers. Curing an attached garage can bring balance to the Life Areas affected, as well as to the entire house.

The garage may be considered separate from the Bagua if there are steps from the main house to the garage, if there is a Run-thru that disconnects the house and the garage, or if the garage has a separate roof line.

Often garages have incoming cars pointing towards an actively used space in the home (Fig. 43). This sends disruptive energy to that living space and could manifest as arguments and irritability while in that room. There is less concern when the cars are directed at a laundry room, closet or mudroom.

For garages that have cars directed towards the living area, placing large heavy items such as tires, riding lawn mowers or filing cabinets between the house and the car is recommended. If there is too little space for objects, a crystal can be hung between the car and the house with the intent to block the incoming energy.

Garages can also be disruptive to activities in the rooms above them, especially bedrooms or rooms where calm focus is important. This can be treated by hanging a

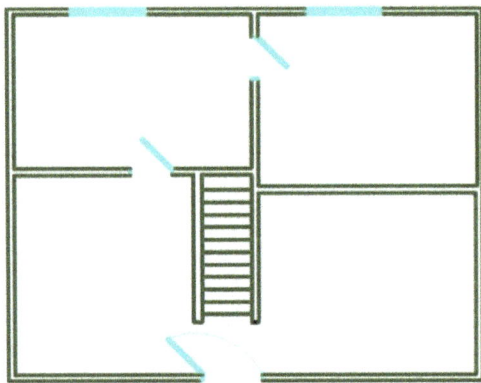

Fig. 44. Stairway Out Front Door

crystal in the garage beneath the room, centered on that room's space with the intent to ground and calm the effect of the garage. Alternatively, a heavy object can be placed in the center of the room above the garage. If preferred, take two heavy objects and place one to either side above the garage entry door in that room.

STAIRWAYS

A stairway is looked at as energy draining out of an area. The most important example is when a second-floor stairway drains down and out the front door, taking with it energy and resources (Fig. 44).

Fig. 45. Stairway Cure

This can manifest as the residents' lacking in vitality and energy or more money going out than money coming in. A basement staircase relates to energy loss in the Life Area from which it originates. For example, a stairway to a lower level that begins in Career could mean trouble with job satisfaction or holding a job.

Cures for stairways are intended to slow down or block the drain of energy. For example, a crystal can be placed centered on the stairs anywhere along its path. Pictures or wall hangings can also be used along the stairway to draw energy up (Fig. 45).

Another cure is a mirror at the top of the stairway, which has the same effect. In the case of a stairway aligned with the front door, a wind chime or crystal can be hung between the foot of the stairs and the front door to stop the drain of energy and resources.

A bathroom situated at the top of the stairs is also a concern. Treat it by hanging a crystal in the center of the bathroom or between the bathroom and the top of the stairs, centered on the stairway.

A homeowner contacted us when her husband was chronically ill and medical bills were draining them financially. When we walked in the front door, the down-rushing energy of the staircase running out the front door showed us at least part of the Feng Shui reason for the owners' troubles. When the cure—a wind chime at the bottom of the stairs—was installed, along with cures to Wealth and Health, there were improvements to the husband's health and the family finances.

Notes

....

....

....

....

....

....

....

....

....

....

....

....

....

....

Notes

....
....
....
....
....
....
....
....
....
....
....
....
....
....
....
....
....
....
....
....
....
....
....

Step 8
Feng Shui the Area
Around Your Home

The key things to consider in the area around your home include the pathway to the front door, the driveway and the Bagua balance of the lot.

Ideally, the pathway to the front door is unobstructed, meandering and attractive to welcome both support and energy to the home (Fig. 46).

To create an inviting entry, begin with clearing things along the pathway to the front door, such as over-hanging bushes and plantings,

Fig. 46. Meandering Entry Pathway

children's toys or overgrowth at the edge of the walkway. To improve the appearance of the area in front of the door, place pots with plants and flowers, lighting or decorative items.

For a home with a straight pathway to the front door, place plantings, lights or pots that alternate along the path to create a meandering effect (Fig. 47). Fix any deterioration in the concrete or stone along the pathway, including broken or cracked steps.

The driveway is analyzed for its welcoming quality or problems with loss of energy. The driveway can be

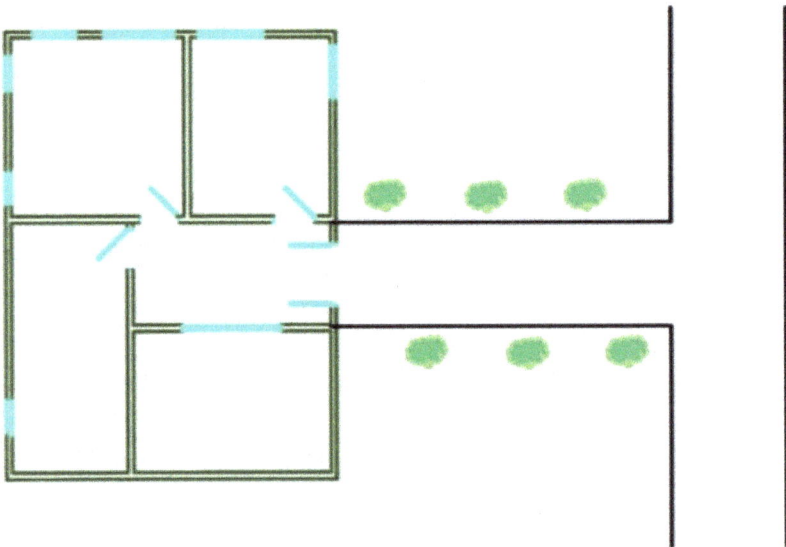

Fig. 47. Pathway Cure

improved in a similar way to the entry path by clearing or removing obstructions along the edge of the driveway.

A driveway that slants downward from the garage to the street can drain or block resources from the home, as well as support for personal goals. It is cured most often by placing larger objects like driveway pillars, rocks, or planters with flowers at the end of each side of the drive-way. This helps hold energy in the property, as well as direct energy to the property. Placing lights, plants, or potted flowers along the driveway can help reduce the drain-out, as well as invite energy to the home.

When the incoming driveway travels past the house and the space ahead of it is unobstructed, it reduces resources coming into the home by guiding them past the house (Fig 48).

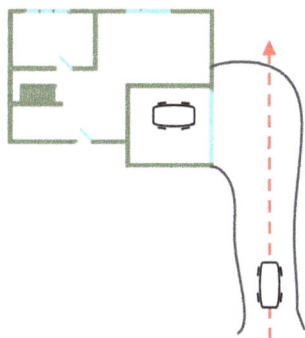

Fig. 48. Driveway Run-thru

Planting trees or placing large rocks or objects in the pathway of that energy will interrupt the Run-thru flow and redirect the energy toward the home (Fig. 49).

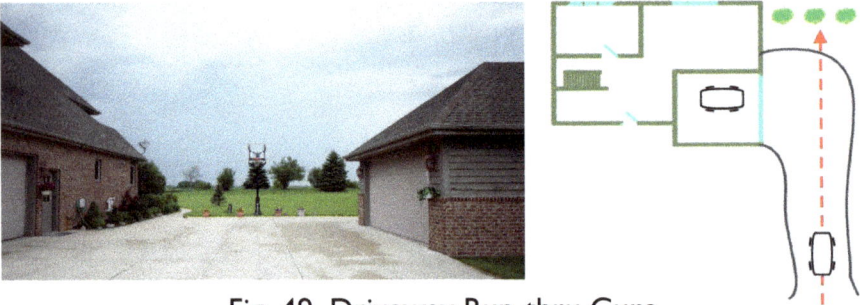

Fig. 49. Driveway Run-thru Cure

As with the home floor plan, the Bagua is placed over the layout of the entire property to determine if there are Missing Areas, Extensions, energetic imbalances or issues in the Key Goal areas.

A Missing Area (Fig. 50) or Extension (Fig. 51) can occur when the lot is an irregular shape. Installing a light, planting trees and bushes, or placing a storage shed or other large objects along the boundary of a Missing Area can reduce its effect. Energizing the area opposite an Extension will bring balance to the lot. Objects such as trees, rocks, gardens, sculptures or out-buildings, and

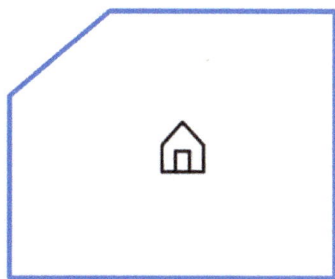

Fig. 50. Lot with
Missing Area

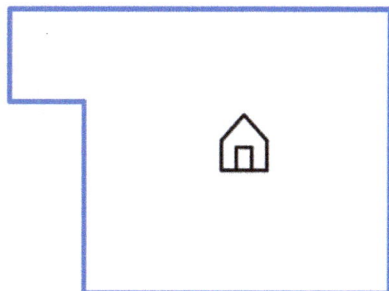

Fig. 51. Lot with Extension

active elements, such as kids play areas or bird-feeding spots, can energize an area opposite an Extension.

In the case where the shape of the lot is regular, these same items can create energetic imbalances if the areas opposite them are empty. These instances can be modified by installing another energetic item in the empty space. For example, if you have a large tree in the Wealth Area and the Helpful People Area is empty, you could set up a bird-feeding area in the empty space.

If you have a swimming pool, fountain or other water element in the Fame Area of the lot, you are bringing water to a Fire Area in the Bagua. This can dampen your reputation. In this case, place some form of the wood element (plants, bushes, trees, wooden and/or rectangular

objects or the color green) near or around the water with the intent to absorb the water. (See Destructive Cycle, Fig. 32 on page 41.)

If the water element is larger, in the case of a swimming pool, a Bagua mirror may be needed, directed at the pool with the intent to send away the effect of the water. (See Appendix A.) Alternatively, a regular mirror can be placed somewhere in the Wealth or Relationship Area of the lot facing the pool with the intent to pull the water element out of the Fame Area.

If the land in a Life Area goes significantly downhill, it could negatively affect goals in that area. Frequently, this occurs in the back of a lot, where it would affect Wealth,

Fame or Relationship by draining money, reducing recognition, or weakening relationships. To cure this, place large objects, including rocks, trees or construction (outbuilding, stone fence, sculpture) at the beginning of a steeper incline and anywhere along an incline that has a more gradual drop-off.

If a property is adjacent to a freeway, a street with fast-moving vehicles, a rapid river, or a railroad track, it can be affected by their fast-moving *chi*, which pulls energy from the property. The best way to manage this is by creating a barrier that separates the property from the effect of the street, river, or railroad. Barriers in the form of trees, shrubs, plantings, large rocks or out-buildings can be effective. Signage placed perpendicular to the pulling energy flow can also help to slow it down.

At times, electrical and cellular poles and towers, along with transformers, can affect the property. Properties next to cemeteries, disruptive commercial property, a Shar chi or difficult neighbors can sometimes benefit from the use of a Bagua mirror to send away any negativities associated with them. (See Appendix A for how to use a Bagua mirror.)

Step 9
Cures, Intentions and Enhancements

CURES

A Feng Shui cure is used to adjust Run-thrus and Structural or Energetic imbalances, to modify negative effects, and to carry a homeowner's intention. Some common Feng Shui cures include crystals, lights, live or silk plants, fountains, and rocks or stones. The following are sample circumstances in which cures are applied.

- A Run-thru can be cured by placing plants or objects along the pathway.

- An Energetic Imbalance is cured by raising the energy of the less active room by hanging a crystal or placing a light in that room.

- A light or a fish tank can be used to energize a room opposite an Extension to cure a Structural imbalance.

- The negative effect of an angled wall can be cured by hanging one or more pictures on the wall.

Choosing which cure to use depends on how severe the issue is. For example, how big is the Missing Area or Extension, and how active or inactive is the space you are balancing?

The bigger or more active an Extension is, the more energized the cure should be. For example, if the Extension contains a busy kitchen, a good cure might be a torchier lamp on a timer for three hours a day. If the Extension contains a quiet study, the opposite area could be cured with a small water fountain.

A large Missing Area might call for a larger-sized crystal cure. For example, a 50mm crystal could be installed when normally a 40mm one would be sufficient. A 30mm crystal might be used in the case of a small bathroom. A long Run-thru hallway may need more than one crystal, plant, or object.

INTENTIONS

Along with curing an issue, a cure can also carry the homeowner's intention for the Life Area in which the cure is placed. The intention is energized by focusing on it during the cure installation process. To energize your intention further, write it down and place it somewhere in the Life Area of the cure. The note can be written on a small piece of paper and placed inconspicuously under a book, lamp, piece of furniture, or behind a painting.

Some common intentions are for better health, increased income, improved relationships, career change, or travel. There could be other levels of intentions that might include help with the following: child custody issues, troubles with co-workers, conflict over money management, depression, sleep disturbances, and weight loss.

The Intention Reinforcement Ritual (see Appendix B) is always used when installing cures in *situations that are problematic* or *include difficult issues*, as in a divorce or serious legal or health matter.

ENHANCEMENTS

Enhancements are used to bring clarification and focus to the homeowner's intent for a specific Life Area. Enhancements are not used to adjust energy like cures are. They are to be used after the home has been harmoniously balanced with cures. They will be less effective when added to a home that is not properly balanced.

For example, two lovebird figurines added to the Relationship Area will not be helpful if part of the Relationship Area is missing.

When the home is properly balanced, a homeowner's intention to increase money flow can be enhanced with a symbol of prosperity, such as a crystal vase placed in the Wealth area.

An intent to have people be more helpful could be enhanced by placing a picture of people you know who have been helpful to others in the Helpful People Area.

Placing a well-executed resume in the Fame Area of the home could enhance an intent to attract a new job.

Elements can be used as enhancements. Representations of the Fire element like red-colored objects, triangular-shaped items, and candles can be used to highlight the Fame Area, because it is a Fire element area. Plants and pictures of trees and flowers can also be enhancing because the Wood element feeds the Fire element. (See Creative Cycle, Fig. 31 on page 41).

In a family home, it may be beneficial to enhance the Health and Family area with representations of the Wood element, like plants, green items or rectangular shapes.

It is also enhancing to write out your intention on a piece of notepaper and place it in the Life Area that it applies to.

We have found that writing down your intention or goal in a question format is more successful in actually manifesting what you want. If you are desiring a new car, the question might read, "What would it take for me to easily get my dream car?" If someone is hoping to find a more peaceful life, the question might say, "What would it take to invite and receive more peace in my life?" The question format allows for the focus on intention and facilitates the letting-go process so that goals can be more easily accomplished. Don't attempt to answer the "what would it take…" question, just let go. In the case of something like a legal matter or adversarial situation, consider adding generalized phrasing to your question, like "… for everyone to benefit from the results."

Artwork that relates to the Life Area that it's in can be used as an enhancement, as long as it is placed with intention and relates positively to the Life Area in some way. For example, a painting of children playing in the Children and Creativity Area would be a good choice for someone desiring a family. Existing artwork should be removed or replaced if it detracts from a particular Life Area or intent. For example, a painting of a solitary person

Notes

Feng Shui Plus

Here are some other helpful ideas that can be used along with Feng Shui to help accomplish your goals.

SPACE CLEARING

At times, using Space Clearing can be useful and productive to clear and refresh the area inside the home. You might also want to clear a space when there have been more serious issues like a death, arguments, illness, emotional stresses or before moving into a new home. Oftentimes, bells, drums and other sound instruments are used for the process.

The Epsom Salt Cleanse has shown clarifying and calming results and is something you can do yourself at home. To prepare, obtain a heat-resistant pan and place ¼ cup of Epsom salts in the center of the pan. Saturate the salts with rubbing alcohol. Set the pan in the center of each room to be cleared and ignite the mixture with a lighter or a match, allowing it to burn until the flame dies out. Refill for each room. You can also carry the pan around the room and reach into corners for a more thorough cleansing.

Consider using a hot pad or some protection from the heat. At times, you might also want to consider hiring a professional space clearer to produce more of the results you are after.

NUMEROLOGY

In some cases, it can be helpful to look at the numerology of the home address to evaluate how well it fits with the goals of its inhabitants. For example, 5020 (add the address digits together 5+2) E. Olive St. would be a number 7 house, which resonates with the tone of rest and relaxation and is well suited to owners who prefer a retreat-like atmosphere.

Someone who desires a more active life outside the home may do well to cure the 7 address. How to do this and further discussion on numerology is looked at more in depth in our advanced book. There are numerous articles and books, as well as experts on numerology, all of which can be referred to.

ASTROLOGY

Consulting an astrologer can be helpful in looking for the optimal time to make changes. An astrologer can also help you choose which Life Areas to focus on by viewing the transits in your chart. This can reveal the Life Areas that will have the most support for change at this time in your life. Looking at your astrological chart will indicate which elements you may be lacking or have in excess. You can then add the element you need more of to your home or decrease an element in your surroundings that you have too much of. This can improve your overall well-being.

HOUSE CONSCIOUSNESS

Another idea is that houses have their own consciousness. It may be useful in some way to take this into consideration. For example, if the owner is dealing with a particular health issue and the Health Life Area has been cured with Feng Shui, the owner could ask the home to bring its consciousness to the healing and become a partner in the process.

Notes

....

....

....

....

....

....

....

....

....

....

....

....

....

....

....

....

....

....

....

....

Additional Considerations

OBSERVATION AFTER CURES

The intentions, along with the Feng Shui cures, can reveal results quickly or may take up to three months after the installation. Look for small demonstrations that show that your goals are beginning to be realized. For example, if your intention is for improved health, look for two consecutive days of feeling better. If your intention is improved finances, you may receive an unexpected check in the mail.

Consider also that if difficulties show up, there may be some adjustments to the cures that are needed. Occasionally, there may be an occurrence of what looks like something bad happening after installing the cures. This is often energy releasing as the space and situation come into better balance. For example, if the goal is for more intimacy in a marriage, an argument may break out before the changes settle in.

After the initial cures are installed, look for any results and changes in your goal areas to see if adjustments need to be made. Continue to fine-tune your cures and enhancements until you find the best balance.

RESISTANCE

On occasion, for various reasons, the homeowner or certain family members can be unconsciously resisting some change in one or more of their goal areas. This can manifest as their not wanting to complete cures in certain areas or installing cures incorrectly.

For example, in the case of a married couple, where one of them desires a better job, the other may have fears of losing the relationship if that person moves ahead into a larger world. Or perhaps someone may have a goal to attract a life partner, but the person has unconscious fears about intimacy. Or owners wanting to increase prosperity may sabotage themselves by misplacing a cure due to their feeling of unworthiness. It is helpful for the owner to imagine any areas where that kind of withholding might be occurring and talk about it with someone to release any blocks.

INTERIOR DESIGN

Consider that some interior design efforts can interfere with Feng Shui cures. For example, an interior designer may want to relocate items that are serving to modify a Run-thru or may choose to place a lamp in an area that would disturb the energetic balance. It is helpful to find an interior designer who is willing to work with good Feng Shui principles.

REMODELING OR BUILDING

When remodeling or building a home, Feng Shui would ideally be applied during the design phase of the project. Feng Shui utilized at this point is more effective than cures used later.

OTHER INFLUENCES

Using Feng Shui influences your life in a positive way. However, the degree to which it can help depends also on a number of other factors including your astrology, karma, luck cycle, psychological blocks, cosmic flows, and your unconscious intentions. These items each have their own influence on what will tend to manifest in your life and when.

BEYOND THE BASICS

In real-life settings, there may occasionally be a home where Feng Shui results occur differently than expected. This invites looking beyond the basic considerations covered in this book. For example, in a home with a missing Wealth Area, owners had a positive financial situation instead of money problems. On further study, it was found that the Missing Area was balanced by the dynamic energy of the shape of the lot. Other considerations that go beyond basic Feng Shui are explored in our other books.

Appendix A
Feng Shui Cures

Appendix B
Intention Reinforcement

Appendix C
Things that can Benefit from Feng Shui

Notes

Appendix A
Feng Shui Cures

A Feng Shui cure is used to adjust Run-thrus and Structural or Electrical imbalances, to modify negative effects, and to carry a homeowner's intention. The following list includes some of the cures that are often used.

- Clear Crystal Balls (Fig. 52)
- Plants
- Lights
- Fountains
- Electrical Appliances
- Fish Tanks
- Heavy Objects
- Bagua Mirrors* (Fig. 53)
- Planter Pots
- Rocks and Stones
- Pinwheels
- Area Rugs
- Moving Objects
- Mobiles (Fig. 54)

Fig. 52. Crystal

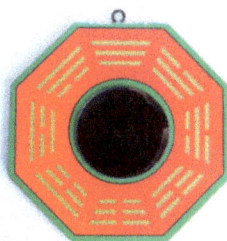

Fig. 53. Bagua Mirror

Fig. 54. Mobile

- Mirrors
- Wind chimes
- Fabric
- Corner Protectors
- Bird Feeders
- Trees
- Sculpture
- Flags

*Please Note—Bagua Mirror:

Since the Bagua mirror can be very powerful, it is used only under special circumstances. It is used to send away potentially harmful energetic effects like large exterior Shars, (see Step 6) cemeteries, issues from problematic neighbors, freeways, cell towers, hospitals, and large commercial buildings. It is always directed toward something outside the home, not directed inside the home. The Bagua mirror can be placed inside as long as it is in a window or on an exterior wall facing outward.

It is important to use the Intention Reinforcement Ritual when installing a Bagua mirror, speaking aloud an intention specifically focused on sending away the negative effect of the item involved.

When purchasing a Bagua mirror, make sure to order regular Bagua mirrors, not concave or convex mirrors, which have special applications. When storing Bagua mirrors, they should be securely wrapped and placed facing downward.

ENHANCEMENTS

The following list includes some enhancements that can be used to focus your intentions:

♦ Artwork

♦ Pictures

♦ Figurines

♦ Meaningful items

♦ Notes with intentions

♦ Symbols for the Life Area

The Five Elements are considered cures when they are correcting an elemental issue in a Life Area. Otherwise they are used to enhance a Life Area. The Five Elements are:

♦ **Earth**—Unglazed pottery, earth-tone colors, square items

♦ **Wood**—Flowers, trees, plants, green colors, rectangular forms

♦ **Fire**—Candles, lights, red, bright orange and yellow, triangular shapes

♦ **Water**—Water items like fountains, blue and black colors, wavy lines and objects

◆ **Metal**—Coins and other metal items, white and silver colors, circular shapes

Pictures or paintings of any of the items above can be representative of the element itself.

INSTALLING CRYSTAL CURES

Hang each crystal on a 3- to 9-inch red string or fishline 3 to 9 inches out from the corner of a room or away from the wall. With a Run-Thru, center the crystal in the pathway somewhere along its length. ***Hang all of the crystal cures at the same time*** to manage the change in energy evenly.

Remember to keep all the cures in place until your goals have thoroughly shifted and you are modifying the Feng Shui for new goals. Hang crystals using the Intention Reinforcement Ritual in Appendix B when there are specific real-life problems that are significant obstacles to your goals, like having a difficult boss when you are trying to reduce stress.

Please Note:
It is important after completing the cure installation process to freely and completely let go, surrender, and turn your goals over to a greater power. Breathe, relax, accept, allow, and receive. Find activities that are relaxing and fun to shift your thoughts away from the desired outcomes for a while.

Appendix B
Intention Reinforcement Ritual

The Intention Reinforcement Ritual is used when installing a crystal cure to add strength to the cure. It is used when curing problematic or difficult situations, like custody battles. Focusing on the intention is what adds strength to the cure. The crystal then acts as an unconscious reminder of the intention. The intentions should relate to the Life Area in which the crystal is hung. Below are the steps to follow.

1. Consider any problems you have that relate to the Life Area of the Bagua. For example, low income would relate to the Wealth area and difficult in-laws would relate to the Health and Family and/or the Helpful People areas and so on.

    Identify the problem(s) out loud and send the issue(s) away by using the flicking hand motion nine times. (Extend the two center fingers strongly past the resisting thumb to flick.) Direct the energy out of the home (Fig. 55).

2. Hang the crystal cure.

3. Recite nine times out loud,
   "Om Mani Padme Hum." This ancient
   mantra is pronounced "Ohm Mah
   Nee Pahd May Hum," and is used to
   enhance the cure with positive value.

Fig. 55—Flicking

4. Think about your intention as if you
   were living it right now. Get in touch
   with how it would feel if your
   intention had already manifested.
   Reach for the energy of what you want to create.
   Express out loud your intention in the best words
   possible. Some sample intentions might be:

   ♦ *Money begins to come to me more easily.*

   ♦ *More people are becoming helpful to me.*

   ♦ *Relationships are growing and developing.*

   ♦ *My health is improving.*

5. Put your intention in the form of this question:
   "What would it take…..?"

For example, "What would it take for me to find a better
job?" or "What would it take to attract a life partner?" or
"What would it take to have more energy?"

Remember to phrase questions so that everyone can benefit
from the result.

Don't attempt to answer the question. Just let it go.

Appendix C
Things that can
Benefit from Feng Shui

People frequently don't consider all the things that Feng Shui can be used for or applied to, often thinking along the lines of creating peace and harmony and more general goals similar to that. Any specific issues related to the nine areas of the Bagua—Wealth & Prosperity, Fame & Reputation, Relationship & Marriage, Health & Family, Creativity & Children, Knowledge & Self-Cultivation, Career, and Helpful People & Travel—are possible considerations. Here are some examples we have worked with:

- Getting support for a lease agreement to come together
- Healing from divorce
- Help getting into a specific college
- Sleeping through the night
- Easing migraines
- Improving pet behavior
- Balancing homework

- Assisting with weight loss
- Getting a new car
- Traveling to specific areas
- Modifying attention deficit disorder
- Supporting health of extended family
- Reducing arguments
- Finding better friends
- Receiving money for specific items
- Helping with letting go and transition
- Increasing number of business clients
- Paying down debt
- Reducing overwhelm
- Getting along better with family members
- Increasing productivity
- Starting a new business

- Decluttering
- Modifying bad habits or addictions
- Enjoying eating healthier
- Exercising more
- Having more free time
- Looking and feeling younger
- Increasing intuition
- Getting more motivated
- Completing a project
- Improving physical intimacy with partner
- Meditating
- Becoming consistent
- Overcoming depression
- Sleeping better
- And many other issues.

About the Authors

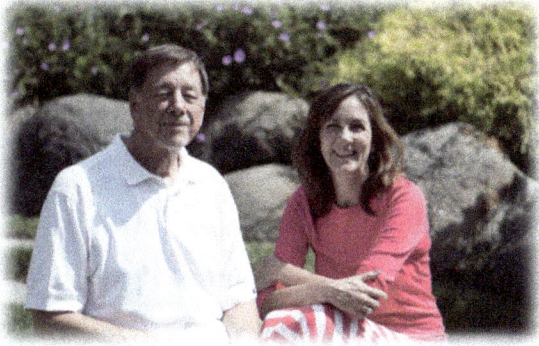

Rhainey Watts-Cunningham and Alex Hartwell are certified Feng Shui professionals who have been practicing Feng Shui since 1998. They draw from extensive training in several different schools of Feng Shui, as well as professional practice in Psychotherapy and Counseling. A strong focus on intention and their personal practices in yoga, meditation, energy work and astrology add dimension to what they do.

Using a team approach, they have found that focusing on certain key areas can serve to accomplish 90 percent of what a client wants from a Feng Shui consultation. Choosing these areas of focus makes looking at Feng Shui less complicated and more manageable. In these areas, they look at how to balance the energy of a home or property so that it facilitates the achievement of their clients' goals and intentions in areas such as Health, Wealth, Relationships, Career, Personal Growth, and Well-being.

Rhainey and Alex operate from the premise that the energy flow in a balanced home or property enhances the life and goals of the occupants. They offer corrections or cures to align the energy of a property with the owner's goals so that those goals unfold more easily.

Rhainey and Alex provide home and business consultations, evaluations for home sales and purchases, consultations for remodeling and building, as well as workshops and presentations. Through their writings, presentations and consulting practice, they intend to help people understand Feng Shui and its impact on their daily lives more easily.

Please contact the authors via their website:
www.Doorwaystoharmony.com

www.ingramcontent.com/pod-product-compliance
Lightning Source LLC
Chambersburg PA
CBHW050017090426

42734CB00021B/3312